YOUR FACADE IS SHOWING

A Divorcees Perspective on Accepting Relationship Red Flags the First Time

DEBBIE L. LONDON

YOUR FACADE IS SHOWING
Copyright © 2018 by Debbie L. London

All rights reserved. Printed in the United States of America. No part of this book may be used or reproduced in any manner whatsoever without written permission except in the case of brief quotations embodied in critical articles or reviews.

First Edition: May 2018

10 9 8 7 6 5 4 3 2 1

ISBN: 978-0-692-12553-3

Convalesce Publishing
P.O. Box 1158
Dallas, GA 30132

debbiellondon.com

This book is dedicated to those who have ignored their instincts when it comes to love and relationships. May it give you the courage to accept what you already know to be true.

TABLE OF CONTENTS

Introduction 9

1: It's Not You 17

2: Examples of Facades 23

3: The "D" Word 35

4: The Aftermath 61

5: Starting at Square One 71

6: Conviction Sucks 83

7: Cutting Your Hand Off 95

8: Connections Can't Be Manufactured 101

9: Loving on Yourself 107

10: Pro-Marriage, Anti-Bullshit 113

11: Cancel the RSVP's 121

APPENDIX 131

Introduction

It is funny how God works and the difference a year makes. If you read my last book, *Residue: Surviving and Overcoming the Stains of Generational Curses and Soul Ties*, you got the breakdown on identifying and starting the healing process from cyclical attachments in your life. Within that book, I talk about how I identified the curses and ties in my own life. I touched on how ridding myself of soul ties led me to my husband. I thought I had it figured out. As someone who is called to heal, I didn't think divorce would be the topic of my next book.

In the middle of writing my last book, God dropped the title "Your Facade is Showing" on me. I'm like, "Lord, why are you giving me a book title when I haven't finished the one I'm writing?" He simply said it would be about relationships. I immediately retreated because I preferred to talk about everything but that. Why? I have always felt people who put out relationship advice tend to have a mess of a relationship or a non-existent one behind closed doors. I didn't want to jinx myself being that I was a mother of two and married for several years.

Now, here we are! The title that was dropped on me makes sense now and I had no idea I would be more familiar with the topic of facades than I would like to be. I mean, I'm whole so I shouldn't make missteps in my relationships, right? I couldn't have been any more wrong! I thought since I was done with f--- boys, became a mother, and got married, I had pretty much absolved myself from unhealthy relationships. My situation was different. There was no drama, no abuse (that I easily noticed), and me and my then husband are great parents. We annoyed each other, but nothing outside of the norm that typically happens in a "healthy" relationship.

Marriage is supposed to last forever, right? In my case it had come to an end abrubtly. What did I miss? What signs did I overlook? How am I going to manage being alone? What did I do to deserve this? Those were just a few of the millions of thoughts that ran through my mind after making a discovery that answered all of the questions I had during the last few years of my marriage. That discovery would also be the start of another healing journey for me. One that I never saw coming.

How do we get into situations that start off so amazing, and then they end in unfathomable ways? When I married, I married for love. I wanted what everyone else did: companionship, support, a life with the person I was meant to be with, children, and building an empire together. I thought I was doing something different when I met my ex-husband. I had a thing for the emotionally unavailable. Being the healing person that I am, I always found myself with people I felt I could fix and eventually create the perfect man out of them. You already know I failed terribly at that. By the time I met my ex-husband, I was tired of the drama and wanted a nice guy. A nice guy is exactly what I got. He was very nice, never disrespectful, but he also wasn't for me. Honestly, I just didn't want to have to deal with the drama of cheating, constantly arguing, and the other turmoil I was used to. When he came along, I thought I struck gold because he was sweet, stable, a good father, and honest.

Isn't it great how we see what we want to in the beginning of relationships? We get so caught up in what we want that we force someone to fit in a spot that wasn't supposed to be there in the first place. We live in the age where everything is showcased. Relationships that look amazing, happy, and fun are considered "goals," but we have no idea what people have going on behind the scenes. We have to be careful looking at the relationships of others and coveting them because you simply never know what they are enduring that you cannot see. When I told people I was getting a divorce they were completely shocked and couldn't understand how something that appeared to be a good thing could go awry so quickly.

I take marriage very seriously. I never wanted divorce to be an option down the road when I got married. I was supposed to be permanently out of the dating game and raising my family in bliss. But, despite our high hopes when we start off in marriage, things can go wrong. When that happens, we cannot just look at the other person. We also need to look at ourselves and own our part in what went wrong. There is so much pressure on being married, having a family, and having the appearance of a perfect life that sometimes we rush into things and make a huge mess. Hindsight is always 20/20!

Weird, huh? A divorced person sharing thoughts to help relationships. Actually, a divorcee's perspective can help you avoid pitfalls and start listening to the voice we often ignore in the name of love. This doesn't mean you will always avoid bad relationships, but you will definitely be able to nip them in the bud quicker. Your decision won't be made because of fear, insecurity, or self-sabotaging, but with common sense and discernment.

I am not a guru by any means (I hate that term). I'm just a servant willing to bare her soul to reassure people like you who may feel alone in what you are experiencing. My goal is simply transforming lives with transparency! I'm your friend that's here to tell you that you aren't crazy, what you are feeling is normal, and most importantly valid!

Come on this journey with me as I describe how we can sometimes miss the warning signs and settle for them because we think we have found the "one." This season of distress will be used to mold and propel you. I was in a low place, but God used that time to show me my reflection in areas that needed healing and correction because they were holding me back. Ready to take off the mask?

Let's Get It!

1: It's Not You

I know some people may scoff at this chapter's title because relationships are not one sided. Typically, both parties can pinpoint areas where each of them contributed to the demise of the relationship. However, that's not what I am talking about here. I am speaking to those of you who have given your all in your relationship. I am speaking to people like you who prayed for and with your partner, treated them the way they wanted to be treated, and still came up empty-handed while feeling alone and unloved. I want to reassure you that your efforts have been honorable, but unfortunately overlooked and will more than likely continue to be. Ask yourself, how long have you been begging your significant other to meet you halfway in your relationship? How long have you felt alone when they are physically there with you? How many times have you made a simple request and they reject it by responding, "This is just how I am?" How long have you asked for their time and communication, yet they find a way to make every excuse for why they can't? How about seeking counseling and still no resolve? Or perhaps they refuse to go to counseling with you?

If you felt some kind of way reflecting on those questions, this is for you. There are people we cross paths with who we are willing to give our lives for, however, they would not do the same for us. At what point do we stop giving our love, time, energy, faith, and trust before we finally have enough and accept the treatment we receive for what it is? It is an incredibly tough realization to know the person we love doesn't love us back or in the way we need to be loved. However, the sooner you realize your differences are contributing to the loss of your sanity and well-being the quicker you need to make a decision accordingly.

In no way am I saying not to work through your issues. Relationships take work, lots of it. I am talking to those relationships where it is 20/80, 30/70, or even 40/60. You are getting less in return than what you are giving. If you are unsure where your relationship falls, make an HONEST list of pros and cons to see which side comes up heavier. I challenge you not to add on the list that you have known them for a long time, you have kids together, they financially take care of you, or the sex is amazing. Those factors tend to skew our view of the person and keep us stuck with them. Get to the root! What is truly good about them and how do they add to your life? What is draining you and causing you to rethink everything constantly? What is helpful to you? What is hurting you? Think about it.

Let me affirm you again and say you have not lost your mind and you are not asking for too much. You are worthy of being loved in the way you need...even if it's not from them. Let me repeat that again, and read it slowly, you are worthy of being loved in the way you need, EVEN IF IT'S NOT FROM THEM. I am all for staying together forever. I really am. However, I think sometimes we are so focused on reaching relationship milestones solely for the sake of saying "we made it" as opposed to saying "we made it AND we are HEALTHY". There is a difference.

    I am guilty of staying with my ex-husband while knowing the warning signs, but I wanted to prove we could make it anyway through emptiness and all. Staying with someone forever while they beat you down physically, emotionally, and spiritually makes no sense and doesn't deserve an honorable mention. Sometimes the person may not be doing anything at all, meaning they don't contribute to your life emotionally, spiritually, and physically in a positive way, which is just as bad. Being with someone who is indifferent about everything is also a problem because they are not helping but hurting you. They are just occupying space in your life literally and figuratively. Everything you have felt is valid up to this point, but what are you going to do about it?

2: Examples of Facades

1

I just think it's funny how (I love that phrase). No really, I do find it funny that at times we meet someone new and decide that instead of being ourselves, we should try to be whatever we think the other person wants. This is dumb and one way a facade forms in relationships. Some people think building a foundation on being the epitome of the perfect mate for someone will somehow garner the perfect relationship. However, you set yourself up for failure every time with this because eventually the weight of not being yourself will be too much to bear. On top of that, you will be resentful toward the person who doesn't appreciate your efforts of trying to be the cookie-cutter version of a spouse they or you want. Save yourself the time and headache and stop doing that crap. There is someone out there who will and can appreciate you for who you are. Don't settle for being a stunt double version of yourself.

2

Other people intentionally hide their flaws out of fear of being judged, not liked, being overlooked, and insecurity. This too creates a facade when character traits that are perceived as a negative quality are hidden for the person to appear more appealing. Once the goal or conquest of "getting" the other person to fall for them is accomplished, they finally "take off their bra after a long day" and let their true selves come forth. My uncle always referred to this as the six-month representative phase.

More times than not, the representative you fell for eventually fades away completely. This new creature then emerges, causing you to question your logic of how you fell for them in the first place. Narcissistic personality types are good with causing you to question yourself. They are the person who always makes it about them. They constantly gaslight you and do everything in their power to make you feel like you are crazy. You will be second guessing yourself constantly with these types because they pulled a switcheroo on you. Ending things with them is even more complicated because you may find yourself going back and forth with them because you are questioning yourself.

They truly don't want anything to do with you. They just want to know they have a little bit of emotional control over you. They may randomly reach out, but then they don't respond to you. They'll sleep with you, but then you never hear from them again. The cycle continues. You deserve more than that. Close all avenues of access for your sanity and peace of mind. Stop praying for peace but entertaining chaos. If that toxic person still has access in your life, you won't be able to make room for the positivity you truly want and deserve. It's time to cut it.

3

Another facade is looking to be the savior in relationships to win pity points when things go awry. For example, you meet someone, they are super sweet and helpful, an all-around genuine person. They offer to do things you never asked for and pull out all of the stops. However, you see over time they only do for others to fill a void in their heart, which makes what they do conditional. They go around talking about how much they do for other people and how things go wrong in their life. They view doing good things for people as a one-way ticket to having their desires fulfilled. This type of person is planting the wrong seeds.

They play the martyr to create the image of an upstanding person who is taken advantage of yet, their spirit is intentionally seeking out broken people to "help." They become distraught when people don't reciprocate the appreciation they want and they sulk about life setbacks from "helping people." They ignore getting to the root of the void they are trying fill, which is the real reason for their lack of progress. You may hear this person constantly say, "I'm a good person." However, if you are truly and purely a good person, you don't have to keep saying it to convince yourself and everyone else.

4

Now, you know what else is a fake front? The idea that relationships will be problem free. When we first date someone everything is beautiful, perfect, and magical. So, we expect the rest of the relationship to be in the same manner. The moment cracks begin to show, disagreements start to happen, or even the slightest bit of skittle glitter wears off...we start to retreat and rethink everything. One thing that is for sure is relationships take work. Work means actually communicating and not feeling like the other person is a mind reader. Work is being patient with your mate's shortcomings and them doing the same for you. Work is listening to your spouse's side for understanding even when you don't agree with it and responding with love. Work is not majoring in the minor things, meaning not finding a reason to nitpick about every, small issue and magnifying it unnecessarily. My generation tires easily. After a couple of failed relationships, we tend to have the patience and tolerance of a person getting their teeth pulled out without anesthesia.

    I accidentally got back on the dating scene after my divorce and this person in particular was great. We had everything in common, laughed, and enjoyed each other's company. Everything seemed to be going fine until remnants of the past began to show up. The parts that came up were showing me a side of him I didn't like. So honestly, instead of trying to work through those issues, I was already done in my head. Why? Because after being married and thinking I knew someone, I couldn't fathom having a relationship with any type of issues like the one we were having. Could I blame a part of that on trust issues? Absolutely. Was I willing to work through that to try to get through those problems? Not really. I just knew in my mind what I could and could not deal with at that stage of my life.

Although in the grand scheme those issues were not unsolvable, I just felt they would open the door to other related issues. Quite frankly, I didn't feel like doing the work. I left us where we were and kept it moving. Do you ever feel like that?

I tried to move the relationship forward a little more and the issues I saw before did become worse over time, so it ended anyway. You and someone can try to work on a relationship, but when it doesn't fit, it just doesn't. The square peg will never fit in the circle!

5

Pretending to be okay with a situation when you really aren't is another facade as well. Let's say you see from the very beginning a person is perhaps a drug user, promiscuous, unsure about moving forward with you, or anything that raises your brow. Why continue with them if those issues are on your radar and deep down you are not okay with them? The quicker you are honest with yourself and stop sacrificing your peace of mind the better off you will be.

It just doesn't make sense to go along with something you know is not a good fit for you. I don't care how good the sex is, how cute they are, or how much potential they have. None of that will matter when the issues you didn't like in the beginning start to drive you crazy later. The other party involved will more than likely not change because they will feel blindsided since you let it go on for so long unchecked. Your sanity is expensive!

Potential is one we are all familiar with. We say to ourselves, if they get a job, get themselves together, stop hitting me, give me attention, and so on...then they will be perfect. I am sorry to relay this to you but relying on potential is the ultimate set up for failure. See, when you stay stuck on potential you are looking for a fairytale (a fake situation to begin with) and completely ignoring what is right in front of you. We have to stop painting people to make them into who we want them to be in our minds. Instead, we need to see the picture right in front of us, with its dull colors, cracked paint, inconsistencies, and other flaws. How many times have we allowed potential to guide us instead of our common sense? I am guilty of doing that more than a few times, but I do not have the energy or time for it anymore.

6

Another type of facade is the one where you don't really know who you are and drag someone else into that chaos. For example, in the African-American community, there are men who are on the down low. To be on the down low means someone lives their life as a heterosexual (i.e. may have a wife and children), but secretly they are homosexual. They do not want to accept it and live their life that way publicly. This is a huge problem for many reasons. The first issue is that person is living a lie.

People who stay in heterosexual relationships when they truly desire something else are wrong. If someone desires the same sex, that is perfectly fine, live your life to the fullest. However, to desire the same sex, be married to a woman to cover it up, and cheat with the same sex is, in my opinion, one of the shadiest and most despicable facades there is. Nothing about you is real, and you knew you were beginning a relationship on the wrong foundation. This epidemic of men on the down low continues to worsen. Now I understand, in our community the difficulty of coming out is not typically received well. It is unfortunate that it is still like this in 2018 because people would rather live a whole lie and bring innocent bystanders down with them because they don't feel they can be free. However, it doesn't make it any more acceptable. There are people suffering from incurable diseases, broken hearts, and humiliation because someone didn't love themselves enough to live in their truth. Once a down-low man's secret is discovered, they make every effort to make the woman feel she is the one out of order and must stay to keep their lie going. Sis, if this is you, RUN! This also goes back to my point about staying in relationships just for the sake of saying you are still together. The humiliation, embarrassment, hurt, and shock will fade and you WILL live and move on. It's better to leave now than perpetuate the lie.

My personal facade was using a mask of confidence to hide that I was really broken, devoid of self-worth, and ultimately settling. I never felt like I was good enough for real and genuine love, so I settled for the scraps I could get and that showed in my relationships. If this is you, you don't have to do that. You are worth so much more. You don't have to hide behind the mask of insecurity, self-doubt, and unresolved hurt any longer. You deserve the best and it is out there. It is up to you to grab hold of it and receiving that starts within.

What type of facade are you dealing with now? What signs did you overlook?

3: The "D" Word

I got married and was for sure I was out of the dating game. I was elated to be a wife and to embark on a journey spending the rest of my life with the person I thought I was meant to be with. I met my ex-husband at a club in Atlanta in February 2011. I know some of you are thinking, "Uh, of course this was destined to fail...look where you met him." I remember that day like it happened seconds ago. A few months prior, I decided I would no longer actively pursue searching for someone to settle down with. I admit, I was a little bit wild when I was young from college up until that point. However, living the life of clubbing every weekend and entertaining different guys gets old quick. I was no longer the responsibility-free college girl I once was. I have always been a hopeless romantic and decided it was time to stop being a party girl. and dealing with what millennials like to call f--- boys. I immersed myself into work, started grad school and promised myself I wouldn't give anyone else my time unless I was planning to be with them on a serious level.

Fast forward to that day in February when a girls night out led to the unexpected moment of meeting the man I would marry. I remember my girls and I happened to run into one of their boyfriends while we were out. He was with his boys and we all decided to hang out together. At this point, I was drunk, enjoying dancing despite the fact I can't (rhythmically challenged) and celebrating having a good life filled with the perks of being an independent woman. A friend of mine pointed out one of the guys from the group and comments on how fine he is. Again, I was drunk and refusing to focus on guys at this point.

However, after mustering up the strength, I realized he had such a beautiful smile, but I didn't care. I was sticking to my plan.

My friend's boyfriend then approached me saying his friend was interested in me. He gave me the rundown about him, saying he was a stand-up guy and they worked together. He then dropped a bomb on me by saying this man was also finalizing his divorce and had a young child. I remember my jaw dropped. One, I had a strong rule about not dating men with children . Two, him getting a divorce was not a good sign considering I promised myself I would only date with the intention of settling down. (Can I just note that we need to stop saying "settle down?" I mean we are practically saying we are working toward receiving less than we deserve from the gate (face palms). So, I said to my friend's boyfriend, "Nah, I'm good," and continued to enjoy myself.

Now, at this club there was an area in the back where you could smoke hookah that had better lighting and you could actually lounge. While walking to the back area, I remember the light hitting the guy's face who was interested in me and I could not believe how breathtakingly handsome he was. Like I had to do a double take because he was indeed every bit of FOINE, do you hear me? He then peeked my curiousity and asked me to sit and chat with him. While we smoked hookah, he immediately let me know he was finalizing his divorce, he was a single father and he showed me pictures of his child. I can't lie, I was even more taken aback he had all that going on. But, I respected him for being upfront from the very beginning and backing what his friend already told me.

He was kind, mature, and different from the guys I previously dealt with. I was also intrigued by how he attractive he was (looks do a play a part). Our group was supposed to meet after the club and get something to eat. He was late meeting us and we were already headed home by the time he arrived. He walked me to my car and asked for my number. I texted him the next day after asking my friend to get his number from her boyfriend. I felt like I had been a jerk by reacting poorly to him being in the midst of a divorce and having a kid. So, I sent him a text apologizing for being rude and let him know I was open to conversing. I sent a paragraph and he replied with a sentence.

     IMPORTANT: This was a sign of what the rest of my life would look like communicating with him. Ya'll 9.9/10 what you get in the beginning of a relationship is what you will get for a lifetime. What issues did you gloss over in the beginning of your relationshp that are now huge? When you look back, you'll see the signs were there all along.

     A couple of days went by and I still hadn't heard from him. I am an alpha female and very impatient. So, I decided to reach out to him. In my true nature, I called him asking why he hadn't called me after having his friend approach me and getting my number. I basically let him know either he was going to talk to me or not. THIS is where the tone was set for the remainder of our relationship. I screwed up right here! If you carefully examine relationships you have been in, you can pinpoint the seemingly small things you ignored. I cannot stress this point enough!

I was the initiator and aggressor from the beginning. He didn't approach me on his own at first, his friend did it for him. I have always gone after what I wanted and in hindsight, I see why that now serves as a problem in my romantic relationships. I never gave anyone the opportunity to really court me because I want what I want immediately instead of letting the man do what he is supposed to. There is much truth in the scripture that says, "HE who finds a wife, finds a good thing." It wasn't meant for us as women to be the seekers. So, let's comb through other things I overlooked in the very beginning, shall we?

He was in the middle of a divorce. I should have probably waited until it was completely final before proceeding. However, he provided me with filing documents, I met the lawyer, and they had been living separately for more than a year so I still moved ahead. Somehow, I believe a negative seed was still sewn in our relationship somewhere during that time. I started seeing more obvious ones once I filed for divorce, so it's hard to say when certain reasons for concern started catching my attention back then. Lastly, perhaps I should not have proceeded knowing he also had a child. As a parent now, I do not think I was mature enough to handle all the things that were dumped on me from dealing with co-parenting issues. Most of my twenties were spent engulfed in drama that I didn't ask to be in, but I proceeded in the name of love.

If you read my book *Residue*, I take you through the origin of the generational curses and soul ties in my life. However, in hindsight I didn't realize I still overlooked my unintentional attraction to unavailable men, even in my own husband. If I am honest, I married him because he was safe. He was not the community dick I was used to dealing with. He was responsible, a good father, stable, laid back, and over games. So, since I wanted to be serious and married, I felt it was only right I got with a man who was different than what I was used to. The kicker is, he was really no different. The common denominator remained the same. Just a different representative. Have you ever experienced that in your relationships? Everytime you are with someone, you get more of the same no matter how much you try. Well, there is a reason for that...your relationships are a reflection of how you feel about yourself internally. For me, my upbringing has something to do with that. I saw so much mistreatment of the women in my family and I wanted to be the one in control. I didn't want guys that could abuse me in the manner I witnessed growing up.

My love language is words of affirmation. This basically means a compliment, a sweet note, or a verbal outpouring of love will send me over the edge. What is crazy is although that is my love language, I have never been with a guy who gives me what I need in that area, at least not consistently and genuinely. Why is that? Because somewhere deep inside of me I believed I didn't deserve to be loved in the manner that I need. How does that happen? How do we go so long without recognizing the patterns and root causes of our behaviors that keep us in a cycle of hurt, disappointment, and chaos? Sometimes it happens because we stick to what we know feels like the safest place to be. We can trick ourselves into thinking, if we let go of that perceived fear of something happening to us, we give it the open invitiation to happen. In actuality, not making the changes to let go of the fears we have will keep us bound to what we don't want.

So back to the story of my ex. Time passed and we had a bit of a whirlwind love in the beginning. It was chill and exactly what I thought was best for me. Whatever I asked of him, he did it for me. He complimented me and he was kind. He even stopped smoking for me although I didn't ask him to. He was the knight to my damsel in distress. Now, fast forward a few months and BOOM, I get pregnant with our son. During the process of my pregnancy, he was great. The issues we encountered were mainly due to the fact I didn't want a man taking care of me. That was an insecurity I had to get over and work through (I discuss that in my previous book as well).

When I actually gave birth to our son that is when everything changed. I take responsibilty for a portion because emotionally I was sent over the edge due to postpartum depression, during which my ex-husband was supportive. I needed that because it helped me unlock my other issues, which lead me to write.

Now, of course when you have kids the dynamic of your relationship will change, duh! However, that is when the work really begins because you have to make an EFFORT to be there for one another. Having a child at that point made me very insecure about not being married. I did not want to have a shot-gun wedding because I think that is silly to do solely because you are pregnant. Too many life changes at once for me, but to each their own who made that decision. However, I did feel out of place for being a mother without a ring on my finger. That internal pressure and wedding fever started to overtake me. That was a red flag on my part because I started high-key bitching to this man about marrying me.

Now, keep it real, have you ever done that crap? Don't lie. No one knows but you and God right now. You have to own that part of your story so you can correct it the next time. It is out of order to try to pressure, pitch, or beg someone to marry you...period! If they want to be with you, they will in their own time. It's important to consider if you're truly being too impatient in your situation. But, if they don't want to marry you yet and you don't want to wait, then you need to decide what your next move is.

So let's press the fast forward button again on this story. We went ring shopping for the second time. At that time, our son was two-years-old and we were together for three years. We just looked at rings to get an idea of what I liked. He picked a ring and I picked one, and then we agreed on the one I liked (I loved that ring by the way!). Maybe two weeks later, God came to me and said, VERY CLEARLY, "Either you want the marriage or the wedding." This was significant because at that point in my life God was shedding me of my materialistic ways (see my previous book for the back story on that).

    I was shocked when God presented me with this ultimatum. I reaallllyyy wanted a wedding, badly. I always have and definitely wanted a memorable reception where we had a choreographed remake of the scene from *House Party*! Yeah, I had it all planned out. However, my ex was anti-wedding. He didn't have one with his first marriage and still didn't want one because they were a waste of money in his opinion. Now I'm hit with this ultimatum. My heart sank and I even cried because I thought, "Dang I really want a wedding, but having a lasting marriage is more important."

    The funny thing about that is God already knew how this would play out. If you know God, you know He is complex and we will never be able to figure out His plans. I ASSUMED since He asked if I wanted the marriage or the wedding, He meant a lasting and loving marriage. The ultimatum did make me realize He wanted me to get my priorities together and stop trying to put on for people. Making that decision helped me in that area tremendously.

    I called my ex and told him what God told me. I let him know whenever he was ready he didn't have to worry about a wedding and the marriage itself was more important to me. He was extremely shocked and couldn't believe I made that decision. I am sure his faith in God grew then (laughs). He immediately bought our wedding bands that evening and proposed to me a few weeks later. In my mind, I was one step closer to the life I wanted. I was a mommy and soon-to-be wife, finally.

    Everything was fine for a while, or so it seemed. I was the vocal one (go figure) in the relationship. Anytime I had an issue, I would make it known. However, he shyed away from conflict. He was an "introvert" and repeatedly told me when I would beg for communication, "It's just the way I am." My future discovery would determine "that was a lie" (in my Maury voice). Listen, when you ask for your needs to be met or request something simple like communication and the one who claims to love you refuses to do it...leave their behind alone. All that begging will only beget more begging, frustration, and negativity until you are just exhausted and numb. Sometimes, when you get excuses from the person about why they can't give you what you need but somehow they can freely do those very things for someone else...interesting.

    I would always be the one initiating (there's that word again) to reach a solution in our arguments. I mean talk about being submissive. I would find books, activities, and do all kinds of things in the hopes of breaking down the walls he had so we could live happily ever after. I mean, that is what a good wife is supposed to do, right? I was always alone in my efforts. He would participate mainly to shut me up.

It came to a point where I started to feel in my spirit he wasn't all in with me. I couldn't put my finger on it, but I felt an unexplainable distance. I KNEW I was more into him than he was into me, but he would always convince me I was being emotional and overreacting. I couldn't shake the feeling and I would say things to him like, "I feel like you don't like me," or "I feel like we are roommates,"or "I swear your guard is up with me." Have you felt like you knew something was off, but you had nothing substantial to prove it? That right there is your discernment alarms going off. We ignore our God-given signals that things are off because sometimes it is easier to remain in denial than deal with reality. Regardless of delay, the pain is going to happen. You might as well face it sooner than waste more of the precious time you will never get back.

However, I don't want you to think distance alone is a reason to leave. Anything can be worked through if BOTH parties come together. You cannot be in a relationship alone. It is like trying to build a house without nails and wood...the shit will never come together. For my people with children, your communication cannot SOLELY be about the household and kids. I get it, we get caught up in the routine of life and sometimes it is like that. It becomes the new normal. When I realized that was happening in my marriage, I became frustrated and bored. Not only that, I became jealous of how he loved and adored our children. Don't mistake what I am saying here. He is an amazing father and our co-parenting is unmatched...I cannot take that away from him. However, I just wanted some attention, any attention from him. To know he could make an emotional connection of some sort made me crave it from him because I felt it was locked away. I thought maybe I just had to do more to get it out of him. Another red flag on my part. You cannot force anyone to do anything. They have to want to do it and make the effort to do so after you disclose what your needs are.

Trying to be a good wife, I started pulling out all the stops. Lingerie, flirty texts, trying to make sure I got dolled up more frequently before he came home from work since I was a stay-at-home mom, and forcing date days. Bruh, that man was not fooling with me. Flirty texts were answered hours later with a response of confusion, not understanding what I was trying to do. Sex became a chore and he never initiated (that word again) it unless I begged him to take control. I remember one time I got dressed and was looking like a meal when he came home from work. I just wanted a simple compliment. One word, "Wow!", would've sufficed. Instead he actually got angry with me for getting dressed up because he said he knew I would want to be complimented. I thought, "Um, what in the entire hell?! Why is showering your wife with compliments and making her feel desired for a split second like pulling teeth?" This incident is probably when I started to feel numb towards my marriage. I just wanted to feel wanted by my husband and he continued to show me I was just a mom and fixture of the household. There was no emotional connection, just routine. I didn't realize or I couldn't put a title on it at the time, but I was being emotionaly neglected in my marriage. Emotional and spiritual connections are, in my opinion, the most important. If those are intact, then the physical and everything else will come together.

Speaking of physical, I love sex! I was happy to be married so I could have sex without guilt. When it got to a point that if I didn't intiate sex it didn't happen, I felt low, ugly, and like something was wrong with me. I understand as parents and in life in general we get tired. Sometimes sleep is going to win some nights, but damn! Him not wanting sex from me and only wanting to lay there while I did all the work was another flag...this dude does not like me. It hurt too much to accept it when I realized it, but I just continued on hoping and praying things would change. I even attributed my actions to the scripure in 1 Peter 3:1, "Wives, in the same way submit yourselves to your own husbands so that, if any of them do not believe the word, they may be won over without words by the behavior of their wives." I thought, "Okay spiritually he is gone at this point. He doesn't want to pray anymore and only sleeps with me to shut me up. Maybe if I continue being a good wife, eventually he will wake up and give me what I need since I am showering him with the love I want in return."

    Outside of him saying I wasn't a good listener (honestly, sometimes I wasn't), he said he had no complaints. I couldn't understand why I was placed outside of his bubble that I wanted so despreately to be in. I wanted to be best friends with him, laugh together, learn his interests and he always said we don't need to do all that. I could not understand for the life of me why someone wouldn't want to be close to their wife. This is why love languages are important. As I mentioned, my top love language is words of affirmation and the next is quality time. I barely got either of those unless I begged for it. I knew what his were and tried my best to show him love in those ways. Utilizing love languages can help couples give each other what they need, but only if both parties are willing and invested in doing so. You can't love alone in a relationship. You will always end up depleted. Have you experienced something like this? Are you currently in a similar situation?

As time went on, my heart grew more weary and frustrated that I wasn't getting what I needed in my marriage. I then asked that we seek counseling, to which he agreed to go with me. I know this is going to sound bad, but you know when someone is doing something not because they really want to but to shut you up? That is basically why he agreed to go, going along to get along. So we went to counseling consistently and I learned a lot about myself because I was open to the process. He was still very closed off and going with the motions, which defeats the purpose. I had some slight breakthroughs that caused me to finally get to a point of surrending in my marriage and accepting that I married an alleged "introvert." If I wanted anything that contributed to an emotional connection, I would have to do all of the work, every time. I was ready to embrace my life and put in the work necessary to continue on as a wife. I had no problem being submissive and keeping the household together, so that's what I did.

Almost a blink of an eye later (I swear it wasn't even a month after accepting the state of my marriage), my discernment was heightened. I saw him receive a text message and attempt to hold back a smirk, to which my spirit let me know something was amiss. Of course, I went through his phone and my suspicions were spot on. I didn't find anything damning, but definitely enough to make me raise a brow in confusion. Little did I know the questions about feeling like roommates, his guard being up, and not feeling like he liked me would soon be answered very clearly.

I confronted him about the text message and even inquired about what I could do so we could communicate better to be more like friends within our marriage. He responded again with "we didn't need to go through all that because we are so different and things were fine as is." Once again, I was shut out and basically told to continue to play my part as wife and mom. I was still very unsettled by that, but pressed on anyway. At this time, I was preparing to launch a personal development tour, which was a nice distraction.

    Now, fast forward to maybe a month and a half later. Two weeks before my tour launched in Atlanta, I made another discovery that answered all my questions I had for years. I ended my marriage and the whole situation almost caused me to catch a case (in my head) in one swoop. Guys, your discernment will never fail you. We can ignore it and try to bury the signals all day, but it will always re-emerge to try to get us to see the light. What I found out was what I already knew in my spirit. I just didn't want to believe it. It was actually hard because initially I never had any concrete proof, just a hunch. You ever know that you know something, but almost sound crazy because you can't really back it up? It is true that if you have to look through your significant other's phone you shouldn't be with them. I had to play detective though because my spirit wouldn't let me rest until the whole situation was nipped in the bud.

Nearly seven years, two children, two miscarriages, and a host of ups and downs led up to this point. My marriage was over. Now I am not going to disclose what I found. I will just let your imagination run free. It was merely the sequel to what I found the first time just more incriminating. I am pro-marriage and pro-love, however, some things cannot be tolerated. There are also some things you just have to accept because there is nothing you can do to change the situation without running yourself in circles knowingly. What is the thing you know right now, but you are choosing to remain in denial about it? What will it take for you to come to a point of acceptance?

The things I found later happened back to back and were basically a continuation of what I found the first time. This time there was no room for denial, it was what it was. The long and short is I confronted him, he saw nothing wrong at first ("How Sway?!"), then later he did see something wrong with it "from my perspective." Do you know how pissed off I was that there was no accountability on his end? Just taking zero responsibilty over his actions and placing it on me. It was mind boggling to me. Just own your shit, say you fucked up and are a fucked up person, and let's go from there.

On top of that, this man I had been with all these years NEVER ONCE fought for our marriage. It seemed as if he was relieved I made my discovery. I actually think he wanted me to find out so he could be free. Do you know how hurtful it is when a person doesn't even try to save the marriage they single handedly screwed up? Seriously, his attitude was like "Welp, you found out and now you're done, so I guess that's it." Never once did he say anything like, "Listen, I know what it looks like, but I am not losing my family over this," or "Whatever it takes, let me show I can make this right." Nope, I got nothing.

I wish I was exaggeratting, but I'm not. But did I need that anyway? He knew the truth and I just found it.

No need to drag it out, I guess. Or perhaps, some people get tired of living a lie and literally have no more energy to contribute to the false image they have created. I would like to think maybe he knew it would only be even more wrong if he tried to get me to stay knowing what we know now. What may seem like the ultimate slap in the face can be the gift you didn't know you needed...peace and freedom!

    Have you had to end something or are you realizing that you need to? What signals have you ignored on purpose?

4: The Aftermath

So, I have taken you through what led up to me divorcing my ex-husband. Now, let me talk about those good ole' emotions that took place afterward. I must talk about them because those emotions are a huge piece that come with acceptance and severing ties with someone. I want to remind you that the feelings you have are valid and you are normal. This is just the process. Actually, divorce is a grieving process. It is a major loss. If you are into psychology, you know grief has five stages. The five stages of grief are denial, anger, bargaining, depression and acceptance.

DEBBIE L. LONDON

When I think back on it, I was actually grieving my marriage long before it ended. Three or so years before it ended I was in the bargaining, depression, and denial phases.

When everything hit the fan, a rage like I had never seen in myself erupted. In the first couple of weeks I was very angry and then in complete shock. I was briefly suicidal at one point and actually had to call the suicide hotline because I was for sure my life was over now that my marriage was finished. Side note: the suicide hotline is very effective. The representative was able to talk me off the ledge and help me get centered. If you ever feel like you need to talk with someone confidentially, please do not be ashamed and get the help you need. You are not alone. I promise! The number is 1-800-273-8255.

Hearing the words from my ex, "You were never asking me for too much," yet he didn't want to do anything to fix it nearly sent me to jail ya'll. The reason that angered me so much is because I BEGGED for years for time, attention, and affection. I begged only to be told I'm too emotional, I'm trying to change him, it's just not who he is, he's an introvert, he isn't a romantic, and he isn't a talker. When the truth comes to light, NOW I ain't asking for too much?? Now my requests were suddenly reasonable because you have been caught? Listen, I told him the worst part of the entire situation was he made me feel like an irrational psycho all these years for wanting to be loved by him. The levy on my emotions broke and I genuinely became fearful I would stab him to death in his sleep. Since I am a mom and I do enjoy my freedom, I asked him to leave the house for a few days. I quickly enrolled myself in counseling to get a handle on the uncontrollable rage I had.

    I felt so played. My heart and spirit knew the whole time I wasn't crazy when I said I felt he didn't like me, that we were roommates, that his guard was up with me, and that he wasn't all in. It is wild to me because he manipulated me into thinking my feelings were invalid and I needed to settle for the way things were. It is upsetting because the moment the jig was up NOW he admitted I was right. He only admitted I was right not because he wanted to make amends, but because now he was finally free. BULLSHIT x1000. Don't you just hate people sometimes? No consideration for the other person whatsoever or their time as long as you got what you wanted out of the deal. I think the happy family with kids or appearance of one was my ex's thing. I'm sorry...I think I noticed I still have a twinge of wanting to slap him in my system (laughs, only kidding...maybe).

Even with all of my anger, after a couple of weeks he felt I should simmer down about it. That only further pissed me off. I saw a Facebook post that summed it up perfectly, "How can a man expect peace from a woman he has made miserable." Drop ALL the mics on that note. I was like, "Dude, you are going to get every bit of my reckless emotions until I tap out!" Don't put a timer on my grief!

With me now in counseling trying to prevent myself from ending up on an episode of *Snapped*, I still had to prepare for my personal development tour (called The Purpose and Healing Tour). I contemplated cancelling but too much collaboration, money, time, and effort was already invested. I had a moment where I looked up and pitifully asked God, "What am I going to do?" He said, "Do the tour." As a creative, I tend to not know what I am going to talk about or do until I get the idea from God. Anything I post or write regarding my purpose work is ordained by Him. My business partner and I still hadn't come up with the activities we were doing for each of our segments of the tour. It may seem last minute, but I notice God works a little differently with creatives or at least the ones I know. Eventually, it hit me that the way I would open up the healing portion of the tour is by disclosing I recently discovered my marriage was over. God showed me that starting off with such transparency was the only way to get my audience to open up and let their guards down as well. Everything fell into place beautifully. I am still in awe of how that tri-city tour was even pulled off. I was speaking healing to others, but in my personal life everything was falling apart.

After the last city, the emotional armor God had given me fell off. The moment the tour was done, my divorce hit me and I grieved hard! I mentally checked out after I finished the healing portion of the tour in Raleigh. God gave me the energy and resilience to push through for a purpose, to pour into others, then He turned me loose to finish my personal healing process. God is so good, isn't He? We don't think we can do something because of our circumstances, but then He provides the will, strength, people, and provisions to bring it forth as long as we are obedient.

As a side note, if there is something you feel you can't take a leap on regarding your purpose because you feel it's not the right time, think again! The sooner you are obedient and take the first step, God will provide along the way. Trust, I didn't have the money to do a tour. I didn't know how to get started. I didn't even know if it would still happen two weeks before the kick-off. He has you, I promise. Take the leap!

Back to being in counseling. If you are struggling with your feelings, please get professional help. There is no excuse to suffer when there are professionals available to assist you. You can easily find a therapist through your insurance. If the insurance is through your employer, they may have an EAP (employee assistance program) that makes your first few sessions free. If you don't have insurance you can use Google to find ones in your area who work on a sliding scale based on your income. Stop delaying your mental health care! We have too many resources out here to keep putting our peace and sanity on the back burner.

Having a therapist was the best decision I could have made and it expedited my healing process tremendously. I was often shocked at times that I wasn't worse off than I could've been. But then I remembered, I was going through the grieving process years before and didn't realize it. I had many fits of crying and yelling at my ex, somehow wanting him to give me the response I was looking for to no avail. During our final civil conversation about the matter, I gave my thoughts on everything. At the end, I gave him the opportunity to plead his case one final time and fight for our marriage. Do you know this man was SILENT?! I wish I was kidding. He asked me out to lunch to talk about everything one last time, and then had ZERO words to say to me. It was the craziest shit ever. I was stunned. I just said, "You really have nothing to say to me right now?" All he said was, "I'm choking..." and he didn't know why. I was like, okay dude, I fought for this marriage the whole time we have been together and if you cannot muster up anything to fight for me for once, you don't have to. Not that he could anyway.

    I pulled out the notes section in my phone with all of my divorce requirements I wrote down prior to our lunch. It included that I wanted him in counseling, how we would proceed with co-parenting, that I was keeping my last name (because it's pretty and it flows), and how we would split our debts. It was clear from that last encounter he was done and maybe didn't want to accept on his end why that was the case. I knew in my heart I was setting this man free to go live his best life and I would not be a part of it. With my anger finally in check, divorce papers officially filed, and a plan on how we would proceed, I was ready to move on or so I thought...

5: Starting at Square One

Finances tend to be one of the causes of divorce. However, the *aftermath* of my divorce had me in a complete financial wreck. I was in "good wife" mode even after filing for divorce. I was trying to make sure co-parenting went smoothly and that me and my ex were on the same page with our divorce decree. I also came up with a plan to help us transition before we went our separate ways. The plan was basically that we sell our home and rent a place, I would start working again and we would pay off joint debts, then part ways after a year. In hindsight, it may have been unrealistic to think we could live under the same roof considering our divorce would be final long before then. However, I had been a stay-at-home mom and I simply wanted to get my bearings before being out on my own again since I would be starting over completely.

    I now understand the meaning of having your own, married or not. That joint situation immediately leaves you out when the relationship is over. I am all for bringing the funds together, but after this experience I think it's best to still have your own individual accounts. I sold our rings and started funneling the money from my book and tour sales into a separate account, which saved me a little bit.

    I had been struggling with severe anger, understandably, since I knew my marriage was over and started counseling. I knew it would be difficult to remain under the same roof with someone who I randomly felt like killing. I knew living together was also slowing down my healing process as well because every day I had to be reminded of betrayal and humiliation. Despite what I felt, we agreed on the plan to live together after selling the house. One week, I mean ONE week, before closing on the sale of our home and moving into the new place, this dude calls me saying he can't move forward.   All of a sudden he didn't want to live with me. Um, the fuck am I supposed to do with only one week to get myself together??

    The interesting thing is the day before, my sister prayed that I could get on my feet as soon as possible so I didn't have to live with him for long. God sure does know how to answer a prayer, doesn't He? While I scrambled to figure out what to do, my ex called the landlord. He told him we didn't want the place anymore, so now the deposit for the rental was just sitting. The VERY next day I get a call for a job I applied for and was hired on the spot.

    The timing was so crazy, I knew it was nothing but God. This job meant I didn't have to move our son's school or find another daycare for our daughter. It also meant I could claim the rental my ex rejected before it was lost since it was right where I needed to be. Funny how God works... What seemed to be a crazy and chaotic situation started to fall into place. What was humbling for me was needing to borrow money from my sisters, family, and friends and max out every credit card I had to make this move happen. After a month of working, I realized I couldn't make ends meet with what I was bringing in. So, I humbly applied for government assistance. Do you know I was DENIED for all of it because I made too much money? However, the fact remained what I was making didn't cover all of the bills. It's crazy how people who don't want to help themselves find a way to slide through the system to get help. However, some people who genuinely need help and who are actively searching for it are given a hard time. So backwards, but another kick in the tail for your girl.

Fast forward a few months and I realized something may be wrong with me when everyone was checking on me, even people I barely talk to. It made me realize I had been unintentionally "turtling." I was absolutely starting to hate my job. Every week it was something else. I would give my all, produce amazing numbers and still it was not enough. I asked myself constantly, "Lord, why am I here?" I was struggling so bad that sometimes in order to put gas in my car, I had to find a credit card that had at least something on it to fill my tank. When my friend's wedding was coming up, I had no idea how I was going to make it there. This was NOT where I envisioned my life. I was now divorced and felt like a single mom (although my ex more than carries his weight). I felt the weight of rubbing invisible pennies together to do basic things. I had to tell my son his Christmas list must be no more than five small presents, even though I didn't know how I would buy them. I felt inadequate for every job I applied for so I reverted to comfort and threw in some administrative positions I knew I could get. I really felt like I screwed up as I proudly watched my brother receive his degree from one of the most prestigious universities in the south and already have an amazing job offer right out the gate. The fact that I, as his big sis, could offer him no assistance shattered my soul because I'm supposed to be his keeper. He has freely given of himself, but I couldn't do it in return for him. THAT hurt more than anything and reminded me I was running in place, moving backwards and not forwards (or so I thought). I had nothing else under my belt. I couldn't even write this book at that time because I was afraid of what people would think and I was at a creative standstill. This new phase had me hating that my schedule was not my own. I was longing for the time I was a stay-at-home mom and had the freedom and flexibility to pour into my passion. At this point, I would wake up at 5 a.m. trying to work on things related to my purpose. I would get myself and the kids ready to leave home and go to work. I would pick them up, get home by 6:30 p.m., and get them ready for bed all to do the same thing again. I was too tired to work on my dreams because of being immensely exhausted.

    The "team no sleep" mantra is cool and all, but I can't creatively push myself under exhaustion. The writer's block was real and every time I tried to pray about my situation changing, God simply told me, "I told you to write..." I was afraid because I believed even if I finished this book, people wouldn't get it. I was afraid they would think I have lost my mind for sharing so much, and ultimately it won't help me get out of my situation. Was this backwards thinking? Yeah, but honestly my faith was below E and I had the hardest time trusting God because I couldn't see HOW all of this would come together. Divorce changed so much for me from childcare, emotional stability, helping my children adjust, asking my mother to move in with me to help with my children, and just trying to get my footing in general. Have you ever felt completely faithless, drained, and unable to see beyond your circumstance? You are not alone.

Communicating with people too deeply during that season made the reality of my situation hurt so bad. I unintentionally avoided talking because I was ashamed of my life and how badly I was struggling. Someone messaged me one day to check on me and said they missed my affirmations I used to post regularly. That pierced me to my core because I was leaving my purpose work hanging, but I just had nothing to give then.

I realized I had more healing to do from my situation, not just emotionally, but financially I had to heal broken areas. I was at rock bottom and refused to live my life in scarcity and lack anymore regardless of how I got there. I was so depressed and frustrated with my finances more than anything. Things weren't perfect when I was married, but it definitely wasn't like this. Sometimes we have to do an honest inventory on ourselves prior to getting into relationships. I can admit finances were always a sore spot for me. Growing up and never having "enough" caused me to never want to live that way again. However, I ran into lack somehow anyway despite my best efforts. I realize now why that happened since the time I was out on my own prior to my marriage.

Before 2018 hit, I asked God to reveal to me what lesson I needed to learn in this season. I didn't want Him to take the problem away. I wanted Him to break the cycle in me so I didn't have to repeat it again. It was a lesson I was tired of experiencing. He whispered to me days after praying that I am constantly in lack because I try to control everything. He told me I couldn't see beyond my own plans thus meaning I didn't trust Him. I would go into panic, a.k.a. survival, mode by relying on credit cards, loans, and borrowing money to take care of things. I grew up with the mindset that I had to get it done at all costs. That mentality of taking care of things by any means necessary can be helpful, but through my divorce it brought me to the lowest point I've ever been in financially.

I had a scarcity mindset, always operating from a place of fear, which led me to where I didn't want to be time and time again. The divorce just magnified it and before going into the next phase, God was doing some heavy pruning on me. He wanted to ensure I didn't bring my old crap with me, which would ultimately sabotage what He had in store. Things were so out of control that I was forced to trust Him because there was literally nothing I could do with my own hands anymore. Literally, I had to believe He had me covered and would provide the provisions: the job, the connections, the healing, and whatever else I needed to break the cycle.

At times, the pain we are facing is so great that we don't see God is truly trying to bring out a new thing in us. It is comfortable and easy to stay the same and do what we have always done. But if we are praying to be taken higher, we will stifle ourselves if our way of being and prayers aren't aligned. So, He may use divorce, a difficult job, a family issue, loss and so on to force you to make the changes you wouldn't make on your own or were intentionally avoiding.

This is important to the facades we have in relationships. Some people go their entire lifetime without looking in the mirror and examining themselves to see how their unresolved issues not only affect them but the people they are with as well. What areas do you keep hitting a brick wall in? What are the negative patterns in your life? What seemingly positive things that worked for you before aren't working for you now?

Ready to change?

6: Conviction Sucks

So I have a problem with sex. Like I loooovvveeee sex. I have always been a bit hypersexual even at a young age, initially starting off as curiosity. It wasn't until writing this book that I realized my "need" for sex was wrapped up in an unfulfilled void. Sex was my release to feel better about myself. The euphoria of being desired and climaxing topped everything. It even sometimes topped being in alignment with God's will for my life. God couldn't give me an orgasm, hug me, kiss me, and make me feel beautiful. In my mind, physical gratification remained a priority to me, married, in a relationship or single.

While finalizing my divorce, I was angry. Angry at the time that was wasted in my life. I was even more livid the last four years of that relationship were spent with me begging for attention whether it was verbal, physical, and most definitely emotional. So, once I made the discovery that my marriage was over, I was on a rampage to make up for lost time. My hormones were raging with trying to "fix" feeling undesired for so long. I desired to meet a guy who I could have an emotional connection with and get my back blown out as well. Because in my mind, sex was the cure for a broken heart and to replenish the esteem I desperately needed to get through the process of rebuilding my life.

When I say I was on the hunt for consistent penis, I mean it. I tried to arrange things with someone I knew through someone else. He had my requirements, he was well endowed, attractive, and willing to do what I needed done. He came over and, I kid you not, out of nowhere he started to look like and embody the mannerisms of my brother. It was truly one of the hardest situations to explain that I have ever been in. He literally morphed into someone else when he looks nothing like my brother. I immediately knew that was the Holy Spirit letting me know this shouldn't be happening. Spiritually, I have unexplained things happen all the time. Those instances are God's way of trying to get me to stop being an idiot and see that I am definitely out of alignment with Him. Seeing the change in this guy killed anything before it started. I was so grossed and creeped out that absolutely nothing happened with him. I went to sleep and kicked him out of my house.

The next situation was with an old friend I reconnected with. We were already comfortable with each other because of knowing each other for so long, but it never went beyond friendship until this moment. I was ecstatic because I knew this person well, we both wanted the same thing, and I was certain I didn't have to worry about drama. He came over to my place and we just hung out for a bit. Through conversing, we realized we had so much in common. Like it was scary in common. We finished each other's sentences and completely understood each other's corny sense of humor without having to break it down,. We connected spiritually and watched God literally speak to us as we are talked about our purpose journey. I thought, "Um, this was only supposed to be booty call...what is all this??" With all of this happening we moved forward to the physical that evening and it was...very nice! This continued to happen and our connection grew stronger as the weeks passed.

I thought to myself this was the perfect setup. We had an out of this world physical, intellectual, and spiritual connection and everything I needed emotionally was provided. Guess what though? He ended up telling me he didn't expect the connection to be so strong between us and that he would like to explore what this may be a little deeper. He said he would like to stop having sex so we could hear from God more clearly. My reaction was pure anger. Petty right? To me it wasn't. I felt rejected, undesired, and deprived. I just left a "dry" situation via my divorce. Now, I find the perfect person to satisfy my needs in more than one way and he has the gall to get all spiritual on me. Whyyyyy? I didn't want to be good. I wanted sex and lots of it because I <u>DESERVED</u> it after everything I endured with marrying the wrong person and being emotionally neglected for years. Take a look at my behavior. See, sometimes we continue the cycle of chaos in our lives by doing what we want right now instead of looking to the future. Ask yourself, do my actions keep me stuck in the same type of relationships?

    I fought that change in our arrangement tooth and nail. I refused to give up sex for any reason because I deserved to get dicked down as a reward for my hardships. I was so unreasonable. Here we have a guy trying to do things right. He said we can't hear clearly from God about what we are supposed to be if we are blatantly going against His will by fornicating. Was he right? Yes. Did I care? No. I actually prayed and asked

God (because I talk to Him about everything) to let me get a pass this time since it's been a rough year. I crack myself up. I could feel God giving me the side eye. Every attempt I made to "free myself" was blocked because I should not have been doing it in the first place.

Loneliness was the primary reason for being on the quest to have as much good sex as I possibly could. I was used to waking up next to someone every day. Although that situation wasn't ideal, and I still felt alone with my ex's physical presence, to me it was still better than actually being alone.

Shortly after knowing my marriage was over, I felt like to cure myself from going completely insane I had to get to know me better. I began watching porn and masturbating, which is something I didn't do before because I never had to. I bring that up because there are so many people who struggle with porn and masturbation. It got to a point where even that wasn't enough for me. One day, I literally started crying because I felt so disgusting and desperate even with pleasing myself. It just wasn't for me and it reminded me of how alone I was. I have always been the type that if I was horny, I had someone to call and have sex with. Now I am resorting to what I feel are desperate measures. The fact that I had a full breakdown because I couldn't get off one day was another signal I had a problem. I had to get control of that before I ended up down the rabbit hole of trying to fill the void. In this season, God is trying to mute that desire in me to help reshape and refocus me on what was truly important, which is fulfilling my purpose.

    I still struggle with this. It is very hard for me, but I know I can and will gain control of myself sexually. This journey has gone in phases. After having to stop with the last guy I was dealing with due to his convictions, I started doing things on my terms and no longer tried to fill a void. I was having sex because I wanted to, not necessarily from an unfulfilled need. At that point, I was rediscovering who I am and needed the freedom to do so. Was I convicted about it? Absolutely! I ended up having to end things with a different guy who I had a perfect arrangement with due to my conviction. God told me clearly, "He isn't the one and you need to abstain from sex." So, I had to block him on everything with zero explanation. Very hard but it was the only way I was going to stop. I also learned after grieving this person I had a spirit of lust attached to me that I wasn't aware of. I always thought my intense desire for sex was "just how I was." However, after going through a cleansing process and breaking all ties, God revealed my grieving was less about the person and more about the detachment of that spirit. Isn't that crazy? I would not have been able to receive that message and understand myself better if I did not cut ties like I was told to do.

    Abstinence on its own is a journey. I have slipped up twice thus far (this was prior to blocking the guy on everything), but I have learned what my limitations are. I cannot even be around certain people in person whether in public or not. I have to be alone in this journey to gain self-control and be successful at it. Sex also stifles me creatively. God's primary reason for me abstaining is not about getting a man because I don't care about that right now. It is so He can flow through me as a vessel. When I am out of alignment, I am creatively stifled, and my purpose work takes a backseat. When I am not having sex, I am able to knock everything out on my to-do list and ideas just flow like I need them to. Like, literally, my connection to God becomes full of static instead of free and clear. Interesting how that works. The last thing I want to do is be cut off from hearing God clearly. My life depends on hearing from Him, so this sacrifice is actually a blessing.

    I have never been able to abstain before because I never truly believed in why I was doing it. Marriage nor a man was not a good enough reason, nor was remaining pure. However, making sure my purpose is fulfilled is extremely important. Every project I have, books, blog, and so on, cannot be executed in the manner it should be if I am indulging in the things that don't suit me in this season. That for me makes abstinence worth it and I am working very hard to strengthen my discipline in this area. If this is a route you are thinking about taking, you have got to know your "why" because if you don't or don't believe in it, it won't work.

Also, previously I would try not to let my knowingly being out of alignment spiritually keep me from nurturing my relationship with God. I know it sounds backwards, but I know we can tend to shut Him out until we feel like we are "good enough" to get back on track. I have to fight that and am now training myself to keep communication open with Him so He can help me through the process. Do you have issues with sex? Are there voids in your life you are trying to fill through sex? What are those voids?

So, let's talk about heartbreak. For me, once I believed I was ready to date again, it felt like a longing that wouldn't end. I was constantly questioning myself and not understanding why I was stupid enough to open my heart again. I felt like a failure all over again because my marriage was unsuccessful and dating is more of the same. When my relationship with that old friend turned sour, I felt like I wasn't able to stop thinking about him, hoping the relationship could work. But, I knew in my heart no matter what image I painted in my mind, the picture in reality was quite clear. Cutting off a relationship because you see the red flags in the beginning feels more difficult than putting a long overdue end to a relationship you knew would end someday. It feels so abrupt and like there is no closure. I felt stupid for sending text messages knowing no resolution would be reached, but I felt like I couldn't remove him from my heart and mind. What I was experiencing at that time were the effects of a rebound. I hate to call it that, but this is exactly what a rebound is...a whirlwind romance.

Dating sucks! Can we just agree on that?! I am a monogamous kind of girl and enjoy being with one person and growing with them. I honestly feel like I'm too old to be back on the dating scene. It is frustrating and aggravating. The feelings of loneliness are sometimes overwhelming. You aren't alone in that. I have caught myself reaching out to people who I shouldn't have in the name of loneliness. This is also why God wants me to be completely alone at this time as well as embrace this season of singleness and abstinence (which I am doing now). Getting to know yourself is most important after a break-up. You will learn what your new deal breakers are, love on yourself, heal, and be a better you. I am learning a lot about myself and I am making adjustments accordingly. This process has been painful but necessary. It is only becoming clear to me now why everything has transpired as it has in my life.

Have you been in a situation where desperation causes you to make the wrongs decisions? Don't be desperate. Have discernment!

Don't be bitter about love. Be better with your decision making about it!

7: Cutting Your Hand Off

Relationships will have you staying with the wrong person forever because you invested so much time and you don't want to start over. You'll talk yourself into staying because you have kids. You don't want to hear, "I told you so," and you're afraid of humiliation. You fear of how your life will end up. You're worried about finances. You're comfortable. You're afraid it's the best you can do or the pain of leaving appears to be more unbearable than staying. Did I miss anything? We cause more hurt and create more chaos by remaining in situations we know should have ended long ago. Staying only wastes your time by prolonging the inevitable. Is it painful to leave someone you love? Absolutely, but the pain is only temporary compared to the continued damage you inflict on yourself.

Imagine being in a garden. You are amazed at all of the beautiful flowers around you, but there is one flower in particular you are drawn to the most. It happens to be a rose. You are taken aback by the attraction you have to this rose, so without any thought you pluck it from its space. You hold on tightly to this rose because you don't want to lose it in the sea of other flowers around you. Over time, you notice your hand bleeding from the thorns piercing the palms of your hands, but the bleeding isn't enough to get you to release. Time passes and the beauty of the rose begins to fade. It is starting to wilt, your hand is cut from the thorns, and the residue from bleeding is staining your hand. For whatever reason, your initial attraction to this rose causes you to continue holding on to it despite its deterioration and the damage it is causing you. You would have saved yourself time and unnecessary pain had you just left the rose in its place and admired it from afar.

    This analogy speaks to how we get into relationships we know we shouldn't be in due to superficial reasons. Despite the pain the relationship is causing us, we stay because we are stuck on the initial attraction, instead of looking at the facts...the relationship is dead. In our minds we feel stuck, but all we have to do is let go. We think releasing the relationship that no longer or never served us will be more painful than it is now. However, we need to understand holding onto it is doing more damage. We must get out of the mindset that losing a bad relationship will beget more pain when in reality it sets us free. It is a struggle to let go of the toxic person in your life, accepting that it will be a struggle, but doing the work is what will give you the peace you desire. The ability to make that tough decision is all a state of mind.

You will never be enough for the wrong person. No matter what you do, no matter how hard you love, no matter how amazing you are to them, how great your sex is...they will never value you if they are not for you. Stop trying to make something fit that won't. The sooner we except certain things and people are not for us, the quicker we can move on and stop wasting our time. The pain we endure from dealing with people who are not for us is self-inflicted. We must learn that we are harming ourselves when we overlook the signs that show us it is time to move forward. I understand we want relationships to work so badly, but it typically comes to bite us in the end. It's better to rip off the Band-Aid and deal with the pain of the healing process now than it is to deal with it later when it becomes an even larger mess.

What dead relationship are you holding to right now? It is time to save yourself and let go. Create a list of facts about the person that you can read every time you start to miss them. It will quickly serve as a reminder on why you are moving on and that there isn't much to miss about them in reality. It really brings you back down to earth. Stick with the facts, not the fairytale you created!

8: Connections Can't Be Manufactured

Sometimes we completely ignore our intuition when it is yelling, screaming, and putting out APB's for us. Why in the world do we try to force things or make them into something when our heart, mind, gut and spirit are telling us to run the other way? Why do we make every excuse to remain in a situation that makes us uneasy, causes us to make self-compromising decisions, and ultimately puts what we know is right on the back burner?

Perhaps, the reason we stay in those situations is the need to feel loved. Maybe it's the desire for companionship. Maybe it's not thinking highly enough of ourselves to nip issues in the bud early to save ourselves from the inevitable headache of dealing with the wrong person. We hope and wish our gut feeling is wrong, so we stick around, continue to get pissed off, diminish our value and get lost in a situation we know we shouldn't be in. When you see how we go against our God-given discernment time and time again, you must admit, we look crazy. It's much easier to follow the path God shows us and be obedient than it is to resist and go in the opposite direction. We waste a boatload of time because while the map says go from point A to B, we instead take unnecessary routes and still have to go to point B anyway. It's ludicrous!

I have learned through my divorce to stop trying to save everyone. I learned to stop always trying to accommodate the feelings of others. I learned to stop making excuses for people's blatantly wrong behavior and to draw a line in the sand to stop taking people's shit. That doesn't mean with the right person I won't be patient and all of that. The issue is that the representative phase of the relationship just gets us every time because we ignore the ever so prevalent red flags. You are smarter than you think you are...trust it.

There are some people who really believe they have the right to demand changes from people. I don't mean logical changes that improve the relationship. I mean, for example, if you curse and your spouse doesn't like it. Your spouse lets you know and you agree to compromise and dial it back as much as you can. There are some people who may have cursing as a deal breaker, but then continue a relationship with you under the impression you will change for them. This is not the way to go. A deal breaker means it causes everything to come to a screeching halt. If you have deal breakers and have zero flexibility with them, don't continue to date someone thinking they will change for you. This is how we set ourselves up for disappointment and waste time.

Be real with yourself and the person you are with. Either accept their flaws or kindly make your exit if deal breakers are present. It may hurt to cut ties, but it will save you precious time later. This can also tie into unattainable standards you are not required to meet. It's not that serious to have someone be in your life by any means necessary. If they are trying to get you to fit into *their* mold, it's not your responsibility to go along with that.

     There are also some people who intentionally put on a mask in relationships in the hopes of securing the person they know they don't deserve. However, they expect once they have that person things should change. I call those people relationship actors. They feel they are going for a role when pursuing you. Once they get you, they do away with the role it took to attract you and change into someone you would never imagine being with. They continue to use manipulation as a tactic after completely flipping the script on the person they are with. They wait until the person falls for them, and then use the person's love for them as a weapon to attempt to manipulate and control them. For example, they say things like, "If you love me you'll do this," or "If I really meant something to you, you would do what I want you to do." Facades can be a form of abuse too.

The calculated facade of intentionally suppressing who you really are to secure the heart of someone you otherwise wouldn't get is probably one of the worst facades of them all, in my opinion. You know you don't qualify to be in this person's life, so you do everything you believe they want and completely change when you feel they are in deep enough with you. This leaves the other person confused, hurt, and questioning their sanity. Have you known someone who does this?

Before you tuck away those thoughts about the things your gut is telling you…ask yourself, is this something I can live with or will this be a problem later? Don't try to change those things about them, either accept them or do you both a favor and move on. If you bring up the issues they have and they get defensive with you instead of having a healthy open conversation...RUN. It means when it comes up later it will only be worse because they really won't budge and you wasted time on something you already knew would be a problem.

    Being able to walk away when you see red flags is an indicator you are confident, firm on your standards, and know your worth. We often stay in toxic situations when those things are out of balance. I obviously had issues in the self-love department, so I attracted as such. Again, I'm not saying walking away is always the answer. However, if you see major red flags waving in the beginning of a relationship, continuing will only produce more of the same results. That is especially bound to happen when there is an unwillingness from the other party to work through those issues.

9: Loving on Yourself

It wasn't until I was in the final stages of my divorce that I realized I had some serious issues. I started focusing on getting to the core of what I was doing wrong in relationships, how did I end up marrying an emotionally unavailable man, and the patterns I was ignoring in my life. I mean, we can't blame the other person fully when we are the common denominator in our missteps. I am not here to tell people what to do. I am simply trying to help you avoid the pitfalls I made in my life so you don't have to continue the cycle of brokenness. I have recently experienced lack of self-love, bad habits, and sexual desires that were all unresolved issues in my life. When I looked at the source, I also found I was acting in a way that was out of alignment with what God wanted me to do. What I mean by that is I had my own ideas of what my life should look like, what my spouse should look like, and where I should be in the present moment.

If we look at a lot of our mistakes we can pinpoint the exact moment we let our perceived needs and wants guide us instead of first checking if we are in alignment with God. I realize even with jobs I had, things I purchased, and people I had relationships with, I was only thinking about my plan. I never considered if this was part of the plan God has for me. Take a moment and evaluate your own life and ask yourself, is what I'm doing driven by God?

I realize a lot of the things I wanted and thought I required weren't even what my spirit truly needed. Often, when we say we need or want something, if we consult with God (even if it's uncomfortable), we'll see we need to trust what He has for us. In this phase of my life, I realize when I got married I did the opposite with the thought that, "Hey, I just need a nice guy." I never consulted God about what I needed.

Why do we feel we know better than God? We really believe with our little human selves that we know better than Him. We really think our plans are much better because we feel we can see the way we are supposed to go. However, what God has for us is always going to be a gazillion times better. I never wanted to date someone who was short, I never wanted to date someone with kids, I never wanted to date someone with [insert any trivial issue here]. I found out the very thing I needed wasn't in the packaging I always thought it would be. That tends to happen time and time again whether it's with a relationship, a career goal, financial goals, children and the list goes on. I realize if we consult with God and allow Him to lay the blueprint and go step by step and follow Him, we will avoid a lot of headaches.

But, instead we want to do things our way, how we want, when we want.

Relinquishing all control is a huge part of getting out of cycles where we constantly date the wrong kind of people. What I mean by relinquishing control is doing so in a manner that lets God lead you in the right space. I am currently in a space where I have given up sex (personal conviction) for a prolonged period of time. Since I have lost my virginity, I have only gone three months without sex. However, what I was doing was making the same mistakes over and over again. Sex is a distraction for me and hinders me in certain ways. I share that to say I am not perfect! As you have your struggles, I have mine as well. At minimum, we can continue to take baby steps to become the person we are meant to be instead of waiting on the right time to do so. It seems like a huge contradiction from what I shared previously because I am advocating for us to be led by God. As I mentioned earlier I was in a space where I felt I needed to feel free although I KNEW it was against my best interest. Have you ever felt like this?

If only we would just let God lead and guide us in every aspect of our lives. I am not in any way trying to minimize the difficulties of not being in control. Trust me, I am a recovering control freak. However, I need y'all to understand that feeling like you need to pilot your life or that you have a better sense of direction will constantly cause you to spiral out of control. Place your life in the hands of the most skilled pilot that will ever be, and that's with the Lord. As I said before in my last book, I am not a Bible beater. However, I love the Lord and there is nothing I can do without Him and I am extremely sensitive to hearing Him even when I fail to listen. There's just no way we exist without Him. I know everyone is not spiritual or affiliated with any religion. However, I would like to clarify that by letting God lead you, I do not mean just freely sitting back. I mean simply allowing God to direct your path as you take action.

10: Pro-Marriage, Anti-Bullshit

I truly don't want anyone to think because I have highlighted the difficulties of relationships I am against marriage. I love marriage, the good, the bad, and the ugly. Marriage is so beautiful when it is done right and the effort is put in to maintain it. I love gleaning from the wisdom of healthy and successful marriages. Even in my failed marriage, I have learned so much. Although when I was in the thick of it I vowed I would never marry again, I would honestly give it another chance. I feel I have grown so much from the experience and have so much positivity to bring to my next and final husband.

While we are on that, being divorced is not the end all be all. I know when we get married we tend to say my first husband/wife will be my last, all of my kids will have the same father/mother, and a list of absolutes that are not guaranteed. We never know how the story will go, which is why it's said to write your plans in pencil. If you are discouraged from a divorce or break-up, I know you feel like you gave your all and there is no way you could give your time and heart to another person. However, I promise you won't always feel like this. The pain seems unbearable and insurmountable and it may feel like this for a while. Focus on the positive. Shift your attention from dwelling on what went wrong in your head. Don't dwell on what you feel your ex owes you and seeking an apology you may ultimately never get. Make the choice to free yourself from any other thoughts or habits that are causing you to stay in the mental and emotional rut you're in now. How have you grown from the situation? What did you learn? What areas do you need to heal from? How can this and how has this made you a better person? What can be used from this situation to propel you forward? Just a few things to ponder on that are positive instead of harping on the negative and staying in the pit of despair.

Let's focus on discussing the positive side of marriage for a bit. What should a healthy relationship be like? I almost said what should it look like, but in the age of social media, I want to be clear about what I mean. A relationship can look amazingly perfect with what meets the eye, but it is actually rotting internally from what we cannot see. A healthy relationship should be peace...an oasis of sorts. That peace is not just from physical gratification or the fuzzy butterflies of new love. How is this person pouring into you outside of the superficial things? Are they praying with and for you? When you are acting like a brat are they patient to help you see the error of your ways through good communication that corrects you? Are they loving you in the manner you need? Are they such a positive person that they make you want to step your game up? Do their good qualities inspire you to shed old counterproductive habits? Do they allow you to be yourself? Do they encourage you on a spiritual level? Those are just some of the things that are hugely important to a healthy relationship. The fireworks are cool, but how is that foundation though?

The person for you won't let you stay the same. They will force you to look in the mirror and shed the parts of yourself that have held you back from becoming the person you truly are. Some people romanticize finding "the one" so much that they forget outside of the fluffy stuff, having "the one" means having an accountability partner who helps you step into the person you are truly supposed to be. It is a painful, but necessary process to be called out on the not-so-favorable parts of yourself. But, having love and support from the right person will push you to make changes that are for the better. A lot of people are so focused on getting the fairytale with the horse and carriage (in this age, a Bentley and chauffeur) that they lose sight of the foundation of relationships. I have been guilty of that right with you.

What happens when you find out the person you are with has a crap ton of baggage from their past? They don't just have baggage in the sense of exes, but they have high levels of brokenness that shaped them and affect how they are in relationships. Do you take the time to help them heal through those issues or do you bounce? Or is it something you feel you aren't equipped to do in the first place? Decisions, decisions... In my previous book, *Residue*, I discussed in 2012 I had an a-ha moment after struggling with postpartum depression. All of the issues I had that stemmed from childhood came rushing forward to where I could no longer ignore them. My ex-husband brought it to my attention and a close relative helped me peel back the layers to get to the root cause of everything. That was a lot of work, but it was so worth it to release the baggage and unlearn everything to become who I truly needed to be instead of a reflection of my upbringing. In fact, I am still refining who I am constantly. Growth is a continuous process.

In relationships, no one will ever be perfect. We know that but tend to forget when things pop off and the stuff we don't like starts to reveal itself. I'm not talking about dealing with a cheater, abuser of any kind, or anyone like that. I'm talking about, for example, discovering the person you're with has self-esteem issues. After doing some digging with them you realize it comes from constantly being torn down when they were growing up. Now they are unable to believe in themselves in certain areas that affect your relationship. Perhaps, the person is always helping people and feels obligated to do so when it is completely unnecessary. You may learn that stems from them feeling helpless in their past, so that affects your relationship in a negative way. What do you do? Do you talk through those situations with them and hold them accountable to their healing? Do you help them get into counseling? Or do you take the first ticket out because of the overwhelming issues someone may have?

I say, if they are willing to actually do the work to heal it's worth it to stick by them as their accountability partner and support system. But, if you are beating a dead horse because they see nothing wrong with their behaviors, they don't care how it's bringing themselves or you down, then it's time to exit. In those situations, you will essentially set yourself up to deal with what you already knew was an issue. Dealing with relationships requires a high level of discernment and wisdom to keep from getting yourself into preventable circumstances. Hindsight is 20/20 for me. This is the reason why I'm sharing what I've learned with you, to help you simply maneuver and detour as it suits you.

I think it's also important to note marriage is not an accomplishment or something you mark off your to do list. I really believe people place too much stock into being married that it becomes an idol for them. It's amazing to find the person you believe is the one God sent just for you. The problem is people tend to worship the idea of marriage to the point that everything they do during their singleness is centered around attracting or finding their lifelong mate. I mean, that's why they aren't coming to you. You are so focused on this relationship happening, creating all these plans and picturing exactly what this person will be like. You are missing the opportunity to live your best life and focus on being the best you for YOU. Stop worshipping marriage. More times than not, the moment you step back and let God bring you the person without being soooo focused on it, they will come. While you are obsessing, you are further blocking your blessing.

11: Cancel the RSVP's

This season of distress will be used to mold and propel you. I ended the first chapter with this statement and now start the last chapter on the same note. Why? It is the main thing I want you take from the experiences I have shared as you apply them to your own life. I was in a low place, but God used that time to show me my reflection in areas that needed healing and correction because they were holding me back. Knowing your worth is pivotal in every part of your life. If you don't know your worth and become tolerant of things that are not favorable to your growth, then you will be held back. It can be a job that completely attempts to diminish you and have you believing you are less than what you are. You may have a boss who sees your light and stops at nothing to try to strip you down. When they are intimidated by you, they want you to believe you are nothing more than an employee who should keep visionary-like behavior at bay.

The same goes in personal and romantic relationships. If you don't know your worth, you will find yourself settling for all kinds of behavior that depletes you. Situations like that put you on a counterproductive path to who you really are and should become. We have to be careful with what and who we give our energy to. Whatever or whoever we give our energy to should be done stingily. Yeah, like that! Be careful and over-protective because the tricks of the enemy like to find any way to get us off track through the things we perceive as non-threatening. Watch your back and your spirit! Sometimes we are in a cycle and don't even realize lessons that we should've learned a long time ago are being repeated because we haven't gotten the message yet. Are there any areas in your life that seem to keep coming around and you don't know why? It is possible it is a cycle that has not been broken and God is trying to get your attention so you can properly sever it. Being stuck in a negative cycle financially, in relationships, in our minds, emotionally, and so on will have us feeling like little mice in an exercise wheel. We'll work really hard to run from what we don't want but stay in the same place because we haven't changed anything to take us to where we desire to be.

Once we understand and humble ourselves to self-examination, we are able to see what we need to do to break free of the same ol' stuff. For example, I mentioned previously in the area of my finances I realized I was repeating the cycle of scarcity. Once I evaluated how the mentality of scarcity and fear were inviting the lack I didn't want, I started making changes. I cut up all of my credit cards. When I started to branch out in my career, I stopped applying to jobs if I would be overqualified and underpaid. I only went for positions that met my developmental expectations. When I stopped operating with the mindset of doubt and fear, I finally excelled in the manner I should have. Even with writing this book, I dragged my feet a little because of fear of how transparent it is and how it would be perceived caused me to stop writing for a while.

At first, I always felt like I was just in my circumstances without any control over it. However, this entire phase of my life forced me to dig a little deeper and examine the areas that repeated themselves. It hurt me to realize when it came to the things I didn't want in life, I was sending a personal invitation to them time and time again. What are the RSVP's you need to cancel in your life?

This time in your life is also a time to be selfish. You have probably given a lot of your time, energy, and heart to the wrong things and people and now you are drained. The only solution is to reset. Selfishness is typically seen as a bad thing, but in this case, it is your opportunity to do what is best for you completely. That means not obligating yourself to do anything you don't want to do. You don't need to continue with a situation you feel iffy about or settle in general because you don't see an alternative. Selfishness can be a positive part in the healing process. In no way am I saying you need to be an unreasonable jerk. However, it is fair that you do what is best for you at this time. When you are ready you can accommodate the needs of others if you so choose.

Being a mother also makes me have this point of view. I have to be careful of who I invite into my life because I have two little people watching me. They have seen the marriage fail between their dad and I. Thankfully, our co-parenting is unparalleled, so that made the transition and current situation smooth for them. The last thing I want to do is hurt them because of me making poor decisions in my dating life. I want to be able to show them real love and healthy relationships exists because I set the standard for them. I do not want a revolving door of losers around my children. They see everything.

I would compare this phase of my life to getting a small cut and treating it immediately rather than to allow it to fester and turn into an infection. The sooner you take action the more empowered you will feel and the better off you will be spiritually, emotionally, and mentally. Sometimes it is not best to wait and see how things will turn out when you are already see what it is. Waiting is only going to allow the issue to grow later. It's like having a seed for a poisonous plant. You know what type of plant it is, but for whatever illogical reason, you decide to plant it and foster it to grow anyway. Stop watering poisonous things in your life, even if the poison is your own toxic behaviors that keep you in an unhealthy cycle.

What are your limits? What will you accept or not accept? What are your deal breakers? It is time you figure out those things about yourself so you can figure out how to proceed in relationships going forward to avoid making the same mistakes. As I mentioned in a previous chapter, I do not mean doing this in a self-sabotaging or defense mechanism manner. Just knowing yourself well enough to know what you have time for is the basis of all of this.

For example, if you don't want to date someone who is dating other people...DON'T! If you don't want to be in the gray area while someone has to figure out where ya'll stand...DON'T! If you don't want to commit to someone yet...DON'T! If you can't handle the baggage someone has...DON"T! Am I making sense here? You call the shots at this point of your life.

You no longer have to lie to yourself about your previous or current mistakes. Accept them for what they are. Do what makes you happy with freedom and unapologetically. FORGIVE YOURSELF! We all screw up in life but stop dragging your mistakes around with you and use them as wisdom to be and do better. Be open to love again but be smart about it. There is no reason to shut yourself off because things have gone wrong before. Pay attention and use your God-given internal alarm and common sense to guide your decisions. If you don't feel confident and don't trust yourself at this time, wait until you do. It is so empowering and needed at this stage. It is okay to want companionship, but not bad enough to sell yourself short in the process. You have the insight to recognize red flags and how to make a move accordingly.

      With all of that said, remember it's okay to be alone. This comes from someone who has never truly been alone for an extended period of time since high school. I have always had someone in my back pocket whether it was for emotional or physical reasons. I realized I was all over the place and couldn't sit still because I didn't know how to. The fear of being alone and facing loneliness have always haunted me. I felt I NEEDED to have someone around me to make the voids I felt less painful. Have you felt like that before? Do you find yourself in situations like this? In true God fashion, He brought me to a point where I had to make a choice.

I had to choose between running from the fear of being by myself or embracing the idea so I could grow in the way I needed to for the next level.

It's scary to be vulnerable and go on the journey alone, but it's necessary to break free of the habits that got you to where you are now. This season of being alone is important because you are re-discovering who you are post-heartbreak or pre-relationship. We need to know ourselves best before we can embark on anything else and being in solitude is how to do it. Being alone is not a death sentence. I repeat, being alone is not a death sentence! You have come this far, and it is time to do what is best for you. Take your time, be selfish so that you can regroup, heal, and go to God or whatever your faith is so that you can move forward. Listen to the voice within...

Be free and make moves in wisdom! God speed on your journey!

APPENDIX

Residue: Surviving and Overcoming the Stains of Generational Curses and Soul Ties

http://debbiellondon.com/residue/

Made in the USA
Columbia, SC
22 November 2018